spot

AFRICAN ANIMALS

CHEETAHS

by Mary Ellen Klukow

AMICUS | AMICUS INK

tail

claws

Look for these words and pictures as you read.

spots

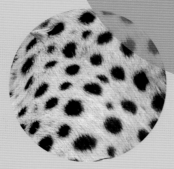

eyes

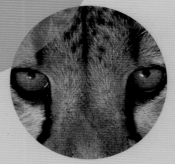

What is that spotted cat?
It is a cheetah!

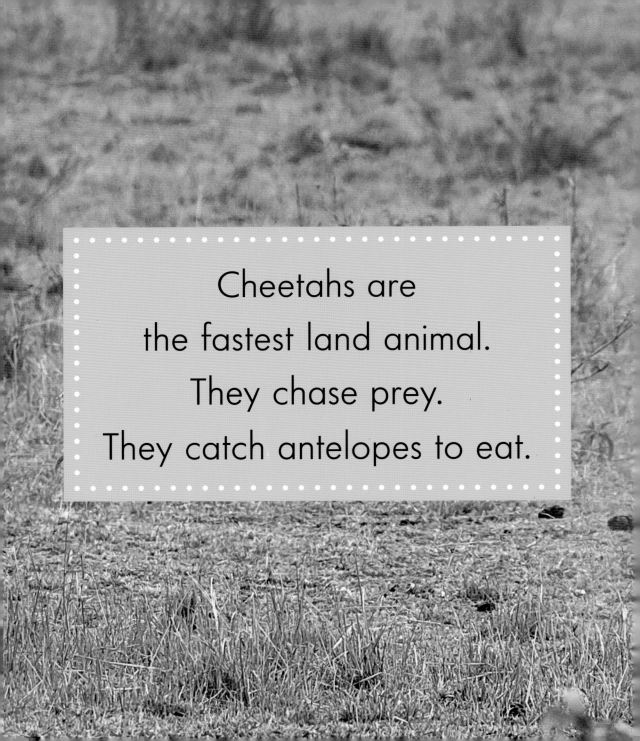

Cheetahs are
the fastest land animal.
They chase prey.
They catch antelopes to eat.

Look at the tail.
It is long.
It helps the cheetah balance.

tail

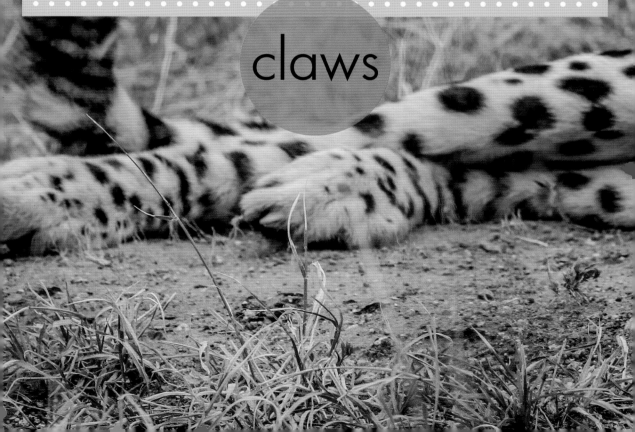

Look at the claws.
Other cats can hide their claws.
A cheetah's claws are always out.

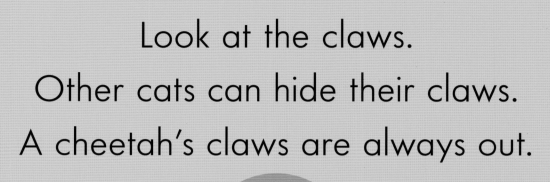

claws

eyes

Look at the eyes.
A cheetah can see well.
It looks for food.

Look at the spots.
They help the cheetah hide.

spots

Baby cheetahs are called cubs.
They watch mom hunt.
Soon they will hunt, too.